# It's Been a Long Journey

---

(Evangelist Victoria Sheffield)

Copyright © 2014 by Victoria Sheffield
Published By Jeru Publications
Cover Photo Credits: Ashley Sheffield

All rights reserved. No part of this book may be reproduced or transmitted in any form or by any means without written permission from the author. Kindle copies can be purchased on Amazon. For more copies, send an email request to sheffieldvictoria39@gmail.com

Chain Breaking Ministries
www.chainbreakingministries.webs.com

# Dedication

I would like to dedicate this book to my Lord and savior Jesus Christ. I dedicate this book to him because without him, the book would not exist. He is the one who gave me the instruction to write this book. He is also the one who gave me the strength to write it.

I also dedicate this book to my family and my church family where Overseer Pastor Anthony Turner & Apostle Mary Turner are my coverings. It was Apostle Mary who gave me a prophetic word about writing this book. That word was also confirmed by my spiritual mom Evangelist Vernell Gabriel.

# Table of Contents

Forward

Preface

Introduction

### **Chapters**

My Humble Beginnings

My First Holy Spirit Experience

Hallelujah I Got Saved

I Hear Wedding Bells

Learning About the Things of God

I Was Called Into Ministry

My Denomination

I Am Sold Out for God

Raising My Children

Spiritual Warfare

Spiritual Encounters

### **Extras**

My Everyday Prayer

A Call to Salvation

Summary

# Foreword

I would like to thank God for the opportunity. I count it an honor and privilege that Evangelist Victoria Sheffield considered me to say a few words about her. I've known her for about twenty plus years. We clicked from the moment we met. One thing I can say about her is that she loves the Lord more than life itself. She was called into ministry and she answered the call. Evangelist has been running the race a very long time. I have seen her tested by God, but never giving up. I can even hear her saying right now that if God said it and I believe it. She is one that truly trust God.

She has been an inspiration to me over the years by showing me that she will speak the truth, meeting you where you are in the flesh and then giving you the bible based truth. I value our friendship because she has always been there through my trying times. She has kept me encouraged even when she was going through. I would not trade her for nothing in the world. I pray that God will bless his people that read this book. Be encouraged!

Nikki Carter

## Preface

In writing this book, I thought about the fact that being a freelance and ghostwriter that i've written many how-to books, curriculums, money saving books, books about business, and articles but have never taken the time to write a book about me and my walk with Christ. I realize as a Christian, I haven't written one book and dedicated it to the Lord. Sure I have authored many spiritual poems and written articles about spirituality but now after all this time, I must write this book so that people can see who I am as a spirit filled woman and where my humble beginnings began. After all, obedience is better than sacrifice.
(1 Samuel 15:22)

With God's help, I wrote about my life's story and how I managed to get this far in this dynamic place of ministry. I wanted to go all the way back to my birth so that my readers could actually get a feel of who I am. I really hope and pray that the book enlightens.

# Introduction

Writing this book has allowed me to open up my life to readers and share details about my intimate relationship with Christ. Writing this was pretty easy. Opening up my life, was not so easy. I realize in my life now that this is not about me. When God taps us on the shoulder, we must learn to move ourselves out of the way and let God fulfill his purpose through us. Jeremiah chapter one says that before the prophet entered his mother's womb, he knew him. The bible also says that many are called but few are chosen. (Mathew 22:14)

I was chosen, ran from the call, and lead by the spirit to write this book. In this book, I share with my readers my first experiences with Christ and my journey living a saved life. The book shares extraordinary details about my gifts of the spirit, how I ran from the call, what made me want to be saved, my birth, how I met my spouse, and details about the birth of my children. I realize now that this gift of sharing my life is just as much of a blessing to me as I hope it will be for you!

Chapter 1

## My Humble Beginnings

I am proud to be a Georgia Peach. I was born and raised in Atlanta Georgia. I am one of four children. I have an older sister and two younger brothers. My parents are from South Georgia. To word it the way it really is, my parents are from the country. Keeping it real, there is no way I can act as if I am snooty or better than anyone else because my entire family on both sides grew up working in the fields as a living. I like to always say that country folks are just plain old down to earth.

It was much earlier in my life that I was made aware by my mother of the hospital that I was born in here in Atlanta. The hospital was called The Holy Family. I was amazed to learn that my nurses were nuns. Now that's being brought into this world in holy presence. Of course that hospital does not exist now but it must have been nice to be born there. As a little girl, I can remember as far back as right before preschool. I remember my first day at school. My mother put me in one of those schools that had a van that would come and pick me up every morning. The school was in this big brick building that was a church. I was so shy as a little girl that I would not talk to anyone. In fact I was so quiet that by the time I entered public school, I was recommended to be placed in a special needs class. My beautiful kindergarten teacher put in a good word for me and told school officials that there was nothing wrong with me. In fact her very words were she is as smart as she can be. She is just over the top quiet.

Throughout my entire time in elementary school I was quiet pretty much and shy. I often got teased and picked on. When I was in preschool, there was this little boy that would pull my hair every morning on the preschool bus on the way to school. I would never fight back. One day out of the blue, I just got tired of being picked on and started fighting back. I went from being picked on to nobody better mess with her. I was about eight years old at that time. I was still quiet and had a few friends but most people I did not say a word to. Now if you were my close friend however, I talked to you all the time.

By the time the summer came after fourth grade, my parents moved from the city of Atlanta across town. I still lived in what is considered Metro Atlanta but the environment was a whole new ball game. I made new friends and was still very quiet. I had a beautiful friend named Deborah that looked at me one day and said girl you are gonna talk to me. It was like she was saying I don't care that you don't talk to anyone else but you are gonna talk to me. She and I became like the best of friends. In fact all these years later we are grown now with our own families but we are still friends. I noticed that where we moved, the children were a little bit nicer. Nobody picked on me and I had more friends. The older I became, I wasn't as quiet but I have always been a mild quiet spoken person and probably always will be.

Now I will share a little bit about me and being brought up in the church. My parents raised us up in a traditional Baptist church in Atlanta, Georgia. My mother and father were both very active in the church. My mother sang in the choir. She lead songs in the choir and my father was a very good speaker. As for my sister and I, we sang in the children's choir. This was a lot of fun because the church that we were a member of traveled locally often because we were invited to many other churches to sing on programs that they were having. We were a huge strong children's choir.

I believe that parents are our first teachers. I feel this way because they are the first people other than sitters or teachers that children have the opportunity to learn from. My mother instilled in my siblings and me how to treat people the way that they should be treated. I saw my father be one of the most responsible providers that any man could be for his family.

The church that we attended was one of those churches where the women would shout after the spirit of God moved them to. They had a baptism pool under the floor right in front of the pulpit. The ministry was very powerful and the church was just a beautiful place to worship. I can remember as a child that my sister and I would laugh whenever a lady would start shouting in church. We didn't know any better. We were just children trying to figure it all out.

I remember being a sweet child. This is not to try to make myself look good. I was never the type of child that got in any trouble or gave my parents any problems. I can remember saying to myself as a child that I never want to mistreat anyone in my life. I truly believe that there are some that are just called and chosen in life. I was a good child and when I look back now I can see that God was letting me know that I was chosen in many ways. I could see things in the spirit and could recognize God in many situations. I noticed as a child that people that mistreated people always seemed to reap what they sow. I saw family members be so harsh and mean to people. I also saw their day of destruction. I was able to see this at an earlier age in my life. When people hurt me I allow God to fight my battles. I am a living witness that we should fret not because of evil doers because they will soon be cut down. If we live long enough, we just may live to see it. (Proverbs 37: 1,2)

Back in my day there was no middle school. Graduating from elementary school and entering into high school was a whole new ball game. I was very active in school. My first year, I was a cheerleader and three of the five years of high school, I was on the drill team. I was even one of two captains of the drill team my last year and elected Ms. Drill team. It was pretty cool to dress up and be a queen at homecoming. The more time went by, I started coming out of my shell more and more. I honestly believe that some of it is heredity. My father is very laid back. One of my baby brother's and a few of my other family members are too.

## Chapter 2

## My First Experience Feeling the Holy Spirit

This part of this book is very detrimental to me because it was at this time about the midpoint of me being in high school that I first felt the Holy Spirit. I can remember being in my parent's kitchen washing dishes. My sister and I shared this responsibility. For some strange reason, I was home alone and I started singing gospel songs over and over again. Even though I was a good person, I was never one into gospel music at all. Somehow I was moved by God to sing one song and then start singing another. Because no one was home, I had no reason to be shy. I simply just opened myself up and sang and hard as I could with all my heart. All of a sudden, I could feel God moving through me. This is all true. It happened in a way that it sort of shocked me to the point where I stopped singing and said to myself, "wow"!

    I knew without a doubt early in my life that God was real.

High school was one of the coolest experiences in my entire life. I had some great friends. In fact we are all still great friends today. I will be honest, before I got saved, I partied until I could not party anymore. I was your average teenager. I liked boys but I was very selective and only dated one boy from my high school. I did not believe in being one of those loose girls. I did a lot of things that I shouldn't have done just like other teens did. I must admit that it seemed as though some of the best times of my life was when I was living in sin. How many of us know that the enemy paints a pretty picture but never seems to show us the real deal until disaster strikes?? To make a long story short, I graduated from high school and entered a technical school by choice because I just did not want to be bothered with a large university.

I started out majoring in accounting and then changed my major to executive secretary or administrative assistant. I just did not want to be bothered with spreadsheets and all those numbers. I was the top student in my shorthand class and decided to drop out of school. I was good at this but felt that sitting behind a desk all day was boring. I decided to lay low for a year and boy was my shorthand teacher and mom a little disappointed.

It was during this time that my family moved to another nearby neighborhood in Metro Atlanta. It was there that I can remember talking to God one day and telling him that I was just at a place in my life where life had no meaning to me. It was as if I was feeling lost. To make it simple, I was feeling alone. My family had stopped going to church and at such a young age, I made the decision to start going back to church by myself. After all I was driving, had my own car, and just needed some guidance. I am just proud to know that at such an early age I made the decision to go to church if this meant by myself. You see I saw what the party life had to offer and wanted to see what God had to offer.

# Chapter 3

## Hallelujah I Got Saved!

One day I decided that I wanted to go to cosmetology school. I finished cosmetology school in eleven months, graduated, and started working in a salon. I was still a party animal. I looked for love in the wrong places. I thought that if I wore short tight dresses to the club that this would land me a real good man. No one told me any different. In all those years of partying, the truth finally hit me. Women that dress a certain way attract a certain kind of man. I could write a book just on the club scene. I witnessed people using cocaine at parties but I knew in my mind that I did not want to go that route. God had his hands on me! Thank God for the blood! You might want to say that I was a good girl in the wrong places. Do I judge people in clubs? Of course not! I am sure that there are some good people in the party scene because I was one of them.

Through brokenness and loneliness, I got saved. One reason I felt lonely is because I had made up in my mind that until God sent me my spouse that I would not date another man. My little brother became my date. He, my niece, and I were born on the same day so we are close as ever. Everywhere I went, I took them but I was still lonely though. People don't fill voids in our lives, God does. What happens next was the best thing that could have ever happened in my life.

    It was a night that I went to bed after parting. I can remember crying with tears rolling down my face and telling God that I was tired. I didn't even know what it meant to be saved. I did not even know that God was about to save me. I just remember telling him that I wanted him to be the driver of my car. I told him that I was lonely and that I could not do this by myself. After that, it felt like a weight had lifted off of me. Many things changed over a period of time with me. When the word of God says that he makes us a new creature, he really does. I had to realize that God does not push himself off on anyone. He is waiting on us to acknowledge him as being Lord and savior of our lives by inviting him into our hearts. Each individual should understand that we cannot go through this life's journey without God.

There were things that he pulled off of me that I did not like. The use of profanity was one of them. This took a while. I can remember visiting a church in the community where I went to high school. Letress a really good friend of mines would invite me there often. I enjoyed this church because the worship was an awesome experience and the choir was strong. The church reminded me much of the church that I was brought up in. I can remember visiting there and when the pastor got to the point where he opened up the doors of the church, I was so nervous. I knew that God was speaking to me about joining. Finally one Sunday I said what the heck, today I cannot let fear stand in my way. Although I was fearful, I joined the church and started singing in the junior choir. I also joined a women's fellowship group that met on Saturdays. This is where I learned about the things of God. By this time, I had given the club life up. It is amazing that God can bring us out but sometimes we try to go back. There was a time when the enemy entered into my thoughts and said you miss dancing, don't you. You see I was one of the hottest things out there and was built like a Coca Cola bottle. So I looked in the mirror and started dancing like I use to in the club. Only this time I felt a little shame and it did not feel as good as it use to. In fact, I even tried to return to the club. The strangest thing happened. After all those years of fun, now when I went to the club it was boring. I mean I could hardly wonder why I ever went in the first place.

Then there was a day that I received a prophetic word from a prophet that knew nothing about my situation that said, God said if you are gonna dance, dance for him. All I will say is that the club life ended on that day for me. I have been dancing only for Jesus every since then. I am in no way saying that dancing or the club life is bad or judging people in a club but what I do know is that God pulled me out. The other word from the prophet was that he did not like the way I was living. What I was gaining from this life was out of the will of God for me. Now he may send someone in there to minister a word to his people but for me, I was not disciplined enough at that time. If God places you in the club to do ministry then so be it but if you go into the enemies camp, put on the whole armour of God. (Ephesians 6:13)

# Chapter 4

## I Hear Wedding Bells

Shortly after I joined the church and got into the Junior choir, I noticed that a familiar face from high school was the choir director. Even though we went to the same high school, we were not friends in school. I do remember a few times that he made advances towards me. He was a year younger than me and played on the football team. I knew of him because I was a part of the drill team and I knew he could sing really well. I will be honest, I brushed him off a couple of times but he was not pushy or persistent. It amazes me when a person becomes new that they can then see things or people that they could not see before. He did show some interest in me again after I joined the choir. At first, I did not think he was my type. I first noticed him one day when he gave a powerful testimony at church. I still never thought that we would connect. The fact that such a young man could testify of the goodness of the Lord really made me notice him. The thing that started drawing me to him was the fact that he knew the Lord.

    Sometimes what God has for us may be totally different from what we would choose for ourselves but his plan is perfect. After that we dated and to my surprise within a few months we got married. He pushed the date up about four months. We chose not to have a wedding. We got married in a church in the same neighborhood as the church we attended. We did not have a traditional wedding. We met the pastor at his church. The three of us were the only people present. Of course, God's spirit was there! In other words we got married for whatever the reason in secret. There were family members that did not like this but this was our choice. One thing I liked about him was that he would call me most Sunday mornings while we were dating just to ask me if I was going to church. All these years later on Sunday mornings he has not changed. He still has that same question on Sunday morning. He enjoyed church just as much if not more than I did. He was pretty much brought up in the church and has many gifts within the music industry. Just a few years ago he was called into ministry and was ordained as a minister. God just keeps on blessing!

Two years later, I gave birth to our first born. This was an exciting experience for the both of us. I always knew I would be a great mother because I have always enjoyed raising someone else's children. In other words, I love children. I practically raised my brother, some of my nieces and nephews, and a lot of other children along the way. At the birth of Samaya, I left my job working in the beauty salon to become a stay-at-home mom. I did not stop doing hair. I serviced clients in my home or theirs. When she turned three I decided to start a Christian Family Home Daycare so that she could be with other children. I never stopped doing hair but the children kept me busy so I did not have many hair clients. I was inspired by God to teach children bible verses, to pray with them, to teach them how to pray, and to teach them the bible. I must say that my home was not your normal home. I saw God move through children and speak through the children that I took care of. Not only did I teach them the bible, I made sure they were prepared for kindergarten. God has given me many gifts of the spirit, but caring for children has always been in the forefront of my life. I notice that I have such a sensitivity for children that it almost seems unreal.

    I must share the fact that when I carried her in my womb, I can remember the Lord saying to lay my hands on my womb and pray. As I prayed for my unborn child, she leaped. I could feel it and once again God did something to get my attention. At that time, according to man the fetus was too young in the womb to even be able to leap but I felt it. The delivery was very hard. In fact the hospital sent me home twice because they felt that I had not dilated enough. The last time, I refused to go home. I prayed and walked around the hospital until she came. Never in life had I been in so much pain. ☺

    My husband insisted on giving her a name. In fact he also insisted on putting her clothes on her in the hospital. So we took this little girl home and I have always been the type of mother that suffered from post pardon depression. When I took my children home from the hospital, I always felt strange. The house felt different and all of the adjusting to the baby and my body feeling different just played with my emotions. In time God makes everything alright.

Chapter 5

**Learning About the Things of God**

So After the baby, the real journey begins. I always enjoyed church and fellowshipping with others. For me, the word was like food for my soul. Regardless of what I dealt with in my life, the word made me feel much better. The more I read his word to this day, it gets better and better. God's word will last through the test of times. I got to the point where I wanted more and more of it. I realized that each individual has to learn over time how to stand on his word. I could feel the presence of God the more I went to church and became more aware about his realm. The more I read my bible, the more peculiar I started to feel. Now that I was saved, I could see more of who I was in Christ and understood more about my calling. There is a whole spirit realm here on earth that represents the kingdom of God. I was so amazed because never before had I experienced prophetic words. The thought of God speaking words to people to give to others was really something. Seeing people speak in tongue was even more interesting. It was as if this whole new way of living was always there but where was I?? I am sure I was somewhere caught up in sin. Thank God for mercy and grace. I thank God that when I got saved he allowed me to ask for forgiveness for the remission of my sins. I did not get baptized at the time I got saved because my mother had us all baptized in the Baptist church that I was brought up in. Today in this place of ministry, I want to get baptized again simply because I do not remember getting this done as a child. This is something that I am getting ready to do in the near future. Remember I wrote earlier that the devil made me think my life in sin was the best thing in the world, but no! Jesus is the best thing that ever happened to me!

Throughout the journey, I joined a women's fellowship group that met one Saturday in each month lead by one of my high school best friend's mother-n-law. It was there and my church that I saw some of the most miraculous things happen. The church I attended at that time was a great church and yes I saw God move and a few prophetic words spoken but it was those Saturday meetings that lasted sometimes as late as 2:00 am because we were having such a good time in the Lord. I saw people being healed of sickness. I saw prophetic words and people speaking in tongues. I saw people shouting, slain in the spirit, and even demons cast out of people. His realm was a whole new ball game for me.

Chapter 6

**I Was Called Into Ministry**

My husband grew up in the church that we attended. A few years after we attended this church, the Lord lead some of his family to start another church. We left our church to become a part of the new ministry. I enjoyed this ministry because it was also there that I learned even more about the things of the spirit. My husband's people were very spiritual people. I learned so much from my mother-n-law, the first Evangelist Sheffield. I thank God for allowing me to meet her. She has never been to Seminary school a day in her life but knowing about the things of God and the way the spirit operates is her calling. I have seen God do so many things through her that I will keep in my memory for the rest of my life. She was also a part of the women's fellowship group I wrote about earlier.

I was different from the people that don't seem to know that they are called until one day they get a revelation. I knew there was a calling on my life but chose to run from my calling. God has a way of letting us know our destiny. At this point in my life, I was growing in the spirit but still considered myself a baby in Christ. I could hear the voice of the Lord and recognize him more and more. Though I was pretty young even friends could see this calling on my life. Ministry comes in different forms but God presented himself to me by showing me that I would preach the gospel. I was very young and excited because I have always loved the idea of helping people in my life but yet the thought of preaching scared me to death. I quickly said no Lord, not me. You have got the wrong one. I am shy and cannot speak in front of people. I mean I would dream that I was preaching and prophets would tell me the same thing.

So the basis of it is that I hid myself working in children's ministries in various churches that I joined. I never liked the idea of speaking in front of people. I was a layed back kind of person that enjoyed keeping to myself. How many of us know that this is not about us? To make a long story short, I stayed in the belly of that big fish walking in disobedience for many years. I lived the life of Jonah for what seemed like forever. God had to allow things to happen in my life to break me. God has to break and mold us so that the oil can flow in our lives. Many things happened but I can only share a few. I will start with the birth of my fifth child. She was born with downs syndrome. When she was six months old, she was diagnosed after the doctor noticed that she had certain features. For me this was devastating. I asked God to take it away because I was scared of the unknown. To me she was just like any other baby. In fact in the doctors own words, "if you are gonna have one like this, you have one of the best ones because they come from being mild to moderate in delays." She was always busy even as a newborn baby. There are things that doctors told me about her that were definitely testers of my faith. By faith, all I can say is that God prevailed. I always tell her that I am stronger because she lives. I could not give up and neither can anyone that is reading this book because trials come to make us strong. They also come that God might get the glory out of our situations.

    Today, Ja'Miracle is eight years old and smart as ever. She has speech delays but she amazes me all the time. I really have to watch her because her immune system can get low and we have had many hospital stays but God delivered us out of them all. I thought she was my last child but God had another plan. I gave birth to another beautiful daughter. Of course the enemy put fear in my heart by trying to make me think that I would have another special needs child. Just to show people how the devil works, I even dreamed while I was carrying her that I gave birth to another child with downs syndrome. In the back of my mind I knew this was the trick of the enemy. After a while I just stopped feeding into the fear.

God gave us what he wanted us to have. A peculiar little girl named Ja'Miracle. Trust me, she is more than the physical eyes can see. When people look at her she is a special needs child but we know that she has many spiritual gifts. In fact all of my children are chosen. They all can see things in the spirit. They all have the gift of discernment and prophecy. I can see other things in them but they all share these same gifts.

I often tell people that I am so thankful that I don't look like what I have been through. I got sick from hypertension and was on high blood pressure medication for three years. I was hospitalized for five days. There were days when I could not walk or drive because I was so dizzy. The medication that doctors gave me made me more sick than the illness. God began to deal with me about that. It was until I decided to fight and truly stand on the word of God that I was healed. This was another test. I first needed to find out why I was sick. I realized that I was sick because I allowed family members to put stress on me. I was also sick because of lack of exercise and poor eating habits. Once I reversed the curse by eating better, exercising, and not allowing people to stress me out, I was made whole again. I have been off of medication for years now.

There are so many things that have happened to me over the years to get me where I am now. I can't write this book and not share this. There was a time when I was asked to speak at an engagement. This was right after I noticed the call on my life. I can remember saying that I was not gonna speak. Somehow I got up the nerve and went anyway. I spoke and the Lord did a great job threw me. I can remember on the way to the church that a car pulled out of no where and almost hit my car so hard but just missed me. After I spoke, I can remember prophetic words going forth from one of the other speakers. Her very words were "somebody in here because you told God what you wasn't gonna do, you almost lost your life in a car accident". All I could do was sit there because that somebody was me. In fact it was that experience with the car that pushed me to get to church faster that day. I was terrified of what could have happened if that car hit me. Yes God will allow things to happen, to get our attention.

Another vision that I had was that I saw an angel forcefully pulling me up to heaven by one of my arms. It was like I had died suddenly and we were ascending up towards heaven. I tried to pull my arm away from him but he would not let me go. It was like he was so strong with might. I can remember this to this day and that was years ago. All I can remember is all of a sudden, I said if you let me go, I will preach the gospel. Then as soon as I screamed that, he let me go and I fell down from the sky. Then I woke up with my heart beating so fast. I was scared but I knew that God meant business for me. Deuteronomy the 28th chapter speaks about the blessings and curses of being obedient and disobedient. If you are reading my book today and you know what your calling is, I urge you to walk into your destiny. Don't be like me because time is winding up. Jesus is on his way back and people need healing and deliverance. The captives need to be set free.

My final draw was when my husband and I lost everything we had. We lost our home, the motor went out in my car and a month later believe it or not his too. We were not as bad as Job but it felt like it. We were both jobless together for the first time. We had no income and six children. Thank God for Jesus. Talk about being tested! So there we were sleeping on my mother's floor down stairs in her lower level of her house. I was able to work for her because she is self-employed. My husband went back to school. We ended up there for a year. We suffered hard and long. God allowed us to be able to fix my car. In the mist of this our marriage was tested. Lack of money is a killer in terms of breaking up a marriage. I realized through a lady that knew our situation, that this was not a time to separate but a time to get closer.

It is sad that some of the people that we had helped all those years were not there for us. If somebody needed help paying a bill we gave them money. Whatever the cause, we were there. Some of the same people that we helped that saw us now down, did not offer us a penny. I can count the few on one hand that did. My question is where is the body of Christ? Little that I knew at the time was that God was birthing a ministry out of me. It was there in my mom's home that my mother actually met a lady that had her own non-profit organization. Not only did she have her own but she helped my mother start hers. When my mother started hers she showed me the ropes. This was something that I had always wanted. In fact I tried in the past years but I just did not have enough money or the resources to be able to bring this to past. God knows our heart and in an appointed time he will give us the desires of our hearts. In all honesty, I still did not have the kind of money that it takes to pull something like this off but God worked it all out. The ministry that helped me and my mother with our non-profit allowed us to break up the fees into payments. This was nothing short of a miracle. All I can say is…ain't God alright! If there is something that you desire to do in life and it just seems like it will never come to pass, I dare you to trust God. Do your part and allow him in his own timing to do the rest. Make sure that it is him that is giving you the vision.

In 2009 God gave birth to my nonprofit Jerusalem Kidz Outreach Ministry. This is a ministry that gives aid to low income families with children. The ministry distributes food and clothing, financial support when funds are available, and gives workshops teaching children the bible and providing fun activities like movie nights, arts & crafts, recreation, fieldtrips & more. We will soon be providing a mentorship program for children. Through all the pain, it all started making since. I have always been very sensitive to the needs of children. I can't express how much I truly love them. All of the pain just meant that I should start this ministry. I once heard the Lord say to me that he made me a mother over nations. I did not know what he meant then but it all came full circle. I feel that when God wants us to do something that we have no peace until it's done.

Of course raising six children has never been easy. My husband and I know what it feels like to have and we know what it feels like not to have much. Just in case you are wondering what ever happened to that Christian Home Daycare that I operated. The daycare stayed active for ten years. After I gave birth to my fifth child, I put in my early retirement from child daycare and started focusing more on my hair and my cosmetic business. I have also launched a fashion & accessory business called Victoria Collection.

    I would love to own a Christian Daycare someday. I will also own my own salon soon. Right now the cost of starting a daycare center is just too overwhelming however not impossible. I will own that center when God sees fit but until then I will continue working with children through my nonprofit organization. I love children and there are those times when I miss working with them. I do volunteer work at schools, with special needs children, and with other children's ministries.

    In this very year (2014), God spoke to my heart yet again. He birthed a new ministry through me. I can remember when he gave me the name and told me what my assignment would be. The name of that ministry is Chain Breaking Ministries. Through this ministry, God sets the captive free. Using the gifts of empowerment and deliverance, God empowers and strengthens by delivering people from their past and present demons. If it sounds powerful, it is.

## Chapter 7

## **My Denomination**

Since our union, my husband and I have been members of five churches. That may sound like a lot but in twenty three years of marriage that is not a lot at all. The church that his family started was the one that we were members the longest. We were a part of that ministry for nine years until God moved us to another ministry. Now after that it has been an interesting ride. Some may judge us and say that we are church hoppers but we are far from that. I am the type of person that when God tells me to move I go. I truly believe that he gave me the title of Evangelist for a reason. I notice that he will send me to a ministry and it seems just when I start getting comfortable, he will pull me out for whatever the reason.

I have always said to myself that if I could describe myself as far as what denomination I am, I would say that I am Pentecostal, Holiness, or Apostolic. Now this was before I joined the ministry that I am a part of now. Because of who I am in Christ, I notice that when I attend certain churches, I get pretty bored or have the feeling that there has to be more to God than what I am seeing. I would also get the feeling that what I was seeing was old news for me. It seems to me that some people are gifted with the ability to know the spiritual things of God. I believe that some people are chosen to be a little bit closer to God than others in the since that they know more of how the spirit operates. Ministries that operate pretty strong within the gifts of the spirit using prophetic words, speaking in tongues, and that operate in healing and deliverance are the ministries that I feel more connected to. I believe that I am one of Gods peculiar people. Seeing things that some see but there are some that don't see the things spiritually that I see.

 I enjoy ministries where a true word is being taught. I absolutely do not believe in a pastor sugar coating the word. I find that too many pastors are people pleasers instead of kingdom builders. I have no problem with demons being cast out of people and people slain in the spirit. Now some people feel that this is just too much. I feel that this is what it takes. The devil is busy and we are living in the last days. After all what's more important, building a church full of people that will bust hell wide open or building God's church??

    I am finally at a church that feels like me. Praise God! Everything goes where I worship. Our worship is strong and we don't mind confronting a demon. If a person walks through our door most of our members are full of gifts that can discern good or bad spirits.

    I am learning a lot and I fit in just well. The spiritual gifts that I operate in are prophecy, I see things in the spirit, I am a dream interpreter, healing & deliverance, the gift of discernment, prayer warrior, and exhorter. Now in all this, I have not received the gift of tongues. It's interesting because I can hear them in my mind but have never spoke in tongues. I have even heard them while sleeping. I do not feel that God gives us all the same gifts but I feel that soon the gift will be manifested because God is dealing with me about this. I notice that every time I come out of a trial or battle God elevates me. Whenever he elevates me, I receive a new gift or my old gifts become stronger. I believe that if I open my mouth and say what I hear then the tongues will flow. No worries in that area though. What God has for me if it's for me will come in his timing.

Today after all the fire that I have gone through, I am sold out for God. I have a bachelor's degree in Evangelism. I am a licensed minister and am currently taking speaking engagements. Unfortunately it took me a long time because I did not believe that I could accomplish the task that was ahead of me. I also allowed myself to be caught up in fear until God gave me this scripture in Jeremiah the first chapter that reads 4- Then the word of the Lord came unto me saying, 5- Before I formed thee in the belly I knew thee; and before thou camest forth out of the womb I sanctified thee, and I ordained thee a prophet unto the nations. 6- Then said I, Ah, Lord God! Behold, I cannot speak: for I am a child. 7- But the Lord said unto me, Say not, I am a child: for thou shalt go to all that I shall send thee, and whatsoever I command thee thou shalt speak. 8- Be not afraid of their faces: for I am with thee to deliver thee, saith the Lord. 9- Then the Lord put forth his hand, and touched my mouth. And the Lord said unto me, Behold, I have put my words in thy mouth. 10- See, I have this day set thee over the nations and over the kingdoms, to root out, and to pull down, and to destroy, and to throw down, to build, and to plant. Now after I read this, chills ran through my body. This sounds so much like me that it literally blew my mind. The only difference was that I was not a child. I was pretty young though. It was probably in my early twenties that I first knew about my calling.

Today I am willing, capable, anointed, appointed, and ready to fulfill my purpose in life. I now believe that all things are possible through Christ Jesus and I know that I am predestined for greatness and when God called me I was already equipped with what I needed. God through pain had to elevate and prepare me for the journey. Now that my spiritual baby has been birthed, I must finish the task until completion.

## Chapter 8

## I Am Sold Out for God

I am at the point in my life that nothing else matters to me than serving the Lord. God is first in my life and I have an excitement about what he is doing in the lives of his people. I realize that all things are possible through Christ Jesus. I can't understand why people are envious when they see God blessing others. When God blesses one he can bless another. My blessing may not be someone else's blessing. His time to bless me may be different from his time to bless the next. The problem with people is that they have not tapped into the fact that we all are blessed. If he has allowed us to see another day then we are blessed. If we have clothes on our bodies, then we are blessed. If we have our health then we are blessed. Being blessed does not always mean we have a new car or house. Even in suffering, we are still blessed.

I often think about just how blessed I really am. My friends are all sold out for God. In fact they love him just as much as I do. Either they are ministers or their gifts are very strong. My friends and I are so close that we pray together and sometimes cry together. If my friends are in need then I am the kind of friend that will help them out and they are the same way. I have no problem with interceding on their behalf and they are pretty much the same.

    Whenever I am going through something that seems very bad, I still believe in giving God praise even when it hurts. My family and I can praise God even when we are going through some of the worse storms. God puts no more on us than we can bare. I feel that we should trust God even when we don't understand and minister to his people in and out of season. God just wants to use us. Regardless of what may come my way, I have made up in my mind that I will serve the Lord if I have to serve him by myself. I have also made up in my mind that I will believe God in his word and hold him to his word standing on his promises.

    I must admit that sometimes we go through things in life that are so overwhelming that we can hardly believe that we are going through so bad. Remember in the book of Job that when he lost everything he had including his children he still worshipped. (Job1: 20) It is in our praise and worship that we are set free, delivered, and healed. We gain the strength that we need to fight. It is like we are saying though he slay me, yet will I trust in him. (Job 13:15) Lord I don't understand this but I know you will deliver and on time. Why because many are the afflictions of the righteous but God delivers us out of them all. (Psalms 34:19)

    Therefore I cannot stress myself worrying about what tomorrow may bring because I trust him with those things I do not understand. In it all, I continue to acknowledge him as being my Lord and savior. I believe that he is in control and that his will be done and release it all to him. Surely once I start truly trusting God is when the peace of God steps in. When I am tired of the journey, I understand this is the point where God carries me. I am so glad that I know that in him I can find a resting place for my soul. It is even better knowing that his glory will be revealed even in this. Sooner or later God always works in our favor. If we can just hold on during the test, they become a testimony. Pain is then turned into power and fear reins with us no more. In fear, doubt, and disbelief

Gods perfect plan in our lives become stagnated. We really have the power to call those things that are not as though they are.

    We must understand that God has a master plan for our lives. We must line our life up with that plan. If we do not we will struggle with an eternal battle of the flesh. It's like we are playing tug-a-war with God. In that battle, there is no peace. That peace and joy will come when we totally surrender to his will for our lives. This is what God is looking for from his church. I am not talking about a building either. I mean his chosen people. I just thought about a football player in the wrong position. Even though he is skilled in what he does because he is in the wrong place, he causes things to go wrong. He is no good for himself or others. He may want to play the position that he is in but this is not the position that he should be in. Because of our human nature we know what we want but God knows what we need. We see in part but he knows the full picture. When we look back over our life particularly at the time when we invited God to come into our lives and take control over our life, we allowed God to come into our hearts and to do whatever it is that he needed to do with us. Why is it when storms start raging in our life, we forget about who he is? He is the same God that fed manna to the Israelites. He is the same God that spoke to Noah about building an ark to save his family. He is the same God that after the army marched around the walls of Jerico for seven days, they fell down. After all it was he that created us and the universe. If he can allow the Red Sea to part for the Israelites, then where is our faith??

Today, I finally get it. Nothing should separate me from my purpose here on earth. In other words no calamity big or small should separate me from the love of God. (Romans 8:39) Even my past should not be an excuse for not walking in the will of God. How many times did I read that but I still did not walk in it? Many! Today I am finally free. This is why I am inspired to write this hoping that someone out there in the world will get this. Please if you are living in the belly of that big fish. Come out in the name of Jesus and walk in purpose. It is until then that any of us will find full joy and peace.

Traveling through this walk of life doing our own thing is like a person chasing wind. It is like never being able to find out where we fit in. I am learning in my life to say and mean, not my will Lord but yours be done. If you are a person that would love to know how you can be delivered from the pain of your past, there is no easy way but there is a simple one. Ask God to give you the strength to press your way through and to show you how to pull down strong holds in your life. The Apostle Paul in second Corinthians chapter ten and verse four says that the weapons of our warfare are not carnal, but mighty through God to the pulling down of strong holds. What we are dealing with on this earth we must deal with in the spirit realm. There really is no other successful way. When I know that I am at war, I read Ephesians chapter six verses ten through twenty. God tells us what we should do but he points out in verse sixteen that above all those things we should do that faith will quench **all** the fiery darts of the enemy.

    You may have to do whatever he is calling you to do in pain but you must fight. You must fight because it is until you are made whole that your full purpose can be fulfilled. Fight the good fight of faith. If people have hurt you, forgive them because the only person that is still be affected by this is you. Notice that people that have hurt you go on with their lives and you are still scarred by your past. I know you may be thinking well I was abused and treated less than a dog. I was raped and talked about. Understand that they abused and talked about Jesus but he came out victorious because he conquered the world. You are more than a conqueror through Christ Jesus. The enemy comes to kill steal and destroy the whole essence of who we are. Even though the enemy has it out for us we really don't have to worry about a thing because he prepares a table before us in the presence of our enemies. The blood that he shed will never lose its power. We should live and set the captive free that his glory might be revealed through us. Sometimes people live a lifetime in bondage wanting change but not having the faith to press towards goals in their life. Successful people in life had the vision and were not afraid to bring their vision to life. There are people right now waiting for us to be free enough to be the people that God has called us to be. God wants to use us to bring forth life in others situations but people need to first see that we are free. How can those chained up unlock the chains of others? It's time to stop living the defeated life and break those chains that have held us captive. People are watching us to see how we handle what we are going through. This is not to say that we should not react to what we are faced with. In reading the book of Job it says that Job reacted to his calamity by tearing off his robe, shaving his head, and fell to the ground. After that, he worshipped. He also said naked I came from my mother's womb and naked I shall return there. He said the Lord has given and the Lord has taken away. Blessed be the name of the Lord. Now we should learn to have an attitude like Job. People should see that we still trust God in everything. In everything we should give thanks. In other words we might be going through but we should still have a praise. God is putting those people in the forefront that people thought were nobodies. He's also waking up everything is us that was once dead. Those dry bones are coming to life.

  The enemy has a way of reminding us of our past but put on the whole armor of God and stay focused. When we begin to stand on the word of God and fight the enemy will not like it. Being held captive in bondage is not the will of God for our lives. The enemy knows what he is up against so he will try everything he can to kill but remember that God is with you when you cross the Red Sea.

# Chapter 9

## Raising My Children

During the early years of my life, I always knew that I wanted to raise my children in the Lord. Even before I birthed my firstborn, I prayed over each child in the womb and God actually allowed me to see them in visions before they were born. I mean when they were born, in most cases I knew what they looked like. I would tell family members about this and they would pretty much think I was crazy until the children were born. A couple of times God would show me what looked like a photo of them when they were much older than a baby. This would be why I say in most cases.

From the time my children were very small children, I would make my children pray together and study the bible together. When my children have what they feel is a problem, I give them a bible based solution. Yes sometimes they feel that I am just too much into God especially the teenagers but that's expected with them. I have made up my mind that if they stray it won't be because they were not taught. I have taught them the word of God. I made sure they were baptized, and I live by example. I do not use profanity in front of my children and I teach them that they should treat people the way that God would require them to. I always tell them that if they do not, then they will reap the benefits of their actions. I have taught them about spiritual warfare and faith. I have also taught them that nothing in life worth having is easy. They know that if they want something out of life that they should work very hard to get the things they want. I am spoiling every one of them but I refuse to spoil them rotten. I believe that if a person spares the rod then they will spoil the child. I also believe that there is such a thing as child abuse. If a few taps on the behind is not enough, then I reframe my children from the television, the phone, or the computer.

    I love my children with all my heart but I refuse to be scared of them and I refuse to be their friends. I am the parent and I expect them to give me the respect that is due. I have never been one to allow my girls to wear short skirts, makeup, or hair color before they reached a certain age because in my opinion, they are just growing up too fast. My oldest that's in college just started wearing skirts shorter than usual because she is out of the house. I just feel that something should be left to the imagination and I am trying very hard to raise virtuous women. I have taught my children how to live right. I have also taught them that they should not have sex before marriage. Now if they choose to do things differently, then who am I to judge but they have to live with the responsibilities that come from having sex before marriage. I am pretty strict about dating but I am open to it as long as they are of age and I can watch them closely without being in their way. I have always been one to tell my children that they could not do a lot of things that they see their friends do. I do not allow everything to go on in my home and I monitor what they watch on television, the internet, and what they listen to on the radio. No Jerry Springer for my kids. I am not big on allowing them to spend the night away from home unless the spirit says it's ok. Academics in my home is a plus. They must hit those books because education is key in today's world.

I made up in my mind that I want them to represent the body of Christ and that's just the way it is. They are not by far perfect but I still must raise them up according to the word of God. I am responsible for them and if I do not raise them right, God will hold me accountable. My children are my first ministry. If my home isn't right how can I minister to other people?

I must admit that raising six children is a challenge. With God's help I can truly say that God has always supplied us with what we need. I have five girls and one boy. To me it seems like it was easier when they were little. Even though they can't do much for themselves when they are smaller, I seemed to get less lip back. Raising teenagers is not a joke. I have a sixteen year old boy. I have a fourteen and soon to be thirteen year old daughter, the daughter in college, a six year old, and my daughter with downs is eight. My children are all gifted in the spirit. They are dreamers. They can see in the spirit and they all have the gifts of discernment. I am sure that I have some musicians waiting to be birthed as well. We may not always agree but we have seen Gods glory and at the end of the day, we are still family.

# Chapter 10

## Spiritual Warfare

One thing I love about writing this book is that I can just be who I am. I mean I didn't even write a rough draft. In all honesty, this book is not so hard to write because it comes straight from my heart. In my heart I truly believe that there is an adversary that wishes to sift us as wheat. Just like I believe in God and his son Jesus, I believe that demons are real. They are so real that I have even seen them. Although they come in different forms that can be very deceiving. I saw one in my sleep once that resembled a beast that tried pretty much to take me out in my sleep. The interesting thing about this is that the demon had points of entry, (fear, doubt, & frustration) this was during a time that I was going through something as we all do at times. I was tired and almost at the point of "I give up". When we are at our weakest, the enemy knows. Sometimes when we are tired we say things we just don't mean. Yes we may be feeling like, I give up or I just can't do this anymore but the worse thing we can do in a storm is take our eyes off of God. When we do this, this allows the enemy to come in and have his way with us. The only weapon that we have is the word of God. This is why we must renew our minds especially when we are tired. Reading the word will get us back on track. After all, nothing should separate us from the love of God. We should not allow fear, problems, or anything that we may be dealing with take our focus off of his promises. Sure because we are human we will get tired sometimes but we must fight the good fight of faith. Sooner or later God will work it all out in our favor. When the enemy whispers to me, I quickly throw the word of God back at him. If I am feeling sick I will say by his stripes, I am healed. If I am feeling angry, I will quickly say God your word says to be slow to anger. There is a verse for anything that we may be dealing with in the bible.

    There is power in the name of Jesus to break every chain. We truly do not have to worry about a thing. Demons are real but so is God. His power is greater than anything the enemy may try to do to us. I am sure that no weapon formed against me shall prosper. Psalms 37:1, 2 says fret not because of evil doers, for they will soon be cut down. This is the very reason why I love to kill people that hurt me with kindness. When people hurt me, they will see it again. In other words, life is full circle. When the enemy is busy, all we have to do is call upon the name of Jesus and speak with authority and demons will flee. It's not something that we should play with either or take light. A demon knows when people fear. It is important to remember that it is not God that is giving us this spirit of fear anyway. Without any hesitation at all, we should use the power that God gives us to bind up any demonic attack that the enemy brings our way. I am good about rebuking attacks over my life. I pray and ask God to help me identify the type of demon that is attacking. Then I simply command them in authority of the name Jesus Christ to go. I make sure that I let the enemy know that I see him and that I am not afraid. I then ask God to replace the spirit that I have cast out with a positive spirit that lines up with Gods will for my life.

    If a demon attacks someone else, and the spirit directs me, in authority without fear, I ask the spirit that is identified to lose that person. Doing this in the name of Jesus is key. If children are present, or anyone vulnerable, then they should be quickly removed from the room or space before ANY of this takes place. We should never lay hands on another person suddenly because demons transfer from person to person. If there is any spirit in me that should not be then I ask God to remove it before I lay hands on anyone. Again, spirits transfer from person to person. This is why it is very important not to allow everyone to pray over us. The enemies will find the weakest vessels to attach themselves to.

Demons are so real that I have even heard them speak. I have heard them believe it or not growl and even try to deceive by chanting that resembles speaking in tongue. I saw just a few Sundays ago my Apostle cast a demon out of a lady. The demon while in her slithered like a snake. In all honestly, I am not afraid of them because I know that all power is in God's hands and he gives us power over them.

I love to read Ephesians Chapter six where it says **10-** finally my brethren, be strong in the Lord and in the power of his might. **11-** Put on the whole armor of God that you may be able to stand against the wiles of the devil. **12-** For we wrestle not against flesh and blood, but against principalities, against powers, against the rulers of the darkness of this world, against spiritual wickedness in high places. **13-** Therefore take up the whole armor of God that you may be able to withstand in the evil day. And having done all, to stand. **14-** Stand therefore, having girded your waist with truth, having put on the breastplate of righteous, **15-** and having shod your feet with the preparation of the gospel of peace; **16-** above all, taking the shield of faith with which you will be able to quench all the fiery darts of the wicked one. **17-** And take the helmet of salvation, and the sword of the Spirit, which is the word of God; **18-** praying always with all prayer and supplication in the Spirit, being watchful to this end with all perseverance and supplication for all the saints.

    Have you ever read certain bible verses over and over but all of a sudden one day you see particular verses in a whole new way? The entire book of Ephesians is awesome. The first verses in chapter six pretty much tell us how to live. Then in verse 10 it says finally after you have done all of the things I say you should do in the previous verses now it is time to do spiritual warfare. When we try to live right, the enemy still attacks! God is so good that he lets us know how we can defeat the enemy. The good news is that we don't have to do this alone. As long as we trust him in his word by putting the word on our situations then no matter how much the enemy tries to come against us, the word of God will prevail. Isn't it amazing that out of all the things that he lets us know we should do that FAITH with quench ALL the fiery darts of the enemy. All of the other things will work as well, but none of them will work if we don't believe. It's about a belief system and putting his word to action.

    David faced a great giant but God was with him. Daniel was in the lion's den but God was with him. Peter starting sinking when he walked on water but God was still with him. There will be times that you will get tired but stay focused when you cross your Red Sea and know that God is with you. Read Mathew 11:28. Come to me all who labor and who are heavy laden, and I will give you rest. It also says in verse **29-** Take his yoke upon us and learn from him, for I am gentle and lowly in heart, and you will find rest for your souls. **30-** For my yoke is easy and my burden is light. I am so glad that when I am tired, I can find a resting place in him. I know this is powerful stuff but I really hope and pray that the next time you are attacked that Ephesians chapter six will come alive in you.

# Chapter 11

## **Spiritual Encounters**

At this point, I think about some of the spiritual encounters that I have had in my life. Of course I cannot share them all because they are intimate experiences between God and I. Some of them are so deep that maybe some will not believe me. I am typing as God leads me so here is what I remember. I remember a time when I was caring for children in my family daycare sitting in my den watching the children play with toys as I watched television. Honestly this blew my mind. All I know is that I was wide awake and I must have just closed my eyes into another realm. As I am typing now, I am even getting chills. This happened many years ago when my oldest children were still little. I can remember seeing a big chair. The chair was a throne. Seated in the chair was God himself. I could see a robe and a crown. Where his face should have been was blurry. I could make this up because I want to sell a book but who do I have to answer to? All I can remember is me standing in front of him. I could see that he was talking to me as if he was giving me instructions about what he wanted me to do while down here on this earth. I could not hear him say a thing. I could only see in this place that he had taken me to that he was talking to me. I could see that there were other people there but they were all blurry. Then I woke up. When I woke up the children were doing the same thing that they were doing before I was taken into that realm. I will be honest, he just closed my eyes in broad daylight for I don't even know how long and gave me this vision.

    I was scared to death and cried like a baby because I knew in an instant what had happened to me. For days, weeks, and even months I was messed up almost not believing that this happened to me. Every time I thought about this, chills and the anointing fell upon me. Over the next few days I wondered what God was telling me to do. Then I began to just seek him. I realized that he was basically just letting me know what my calling was down here on the earth. My calling is to Evangelize. I knew this because he spoke this to me. I had a prophet that knew nothing about me to call me Evangelist Sheffield. If anyone wants to know who I am in Christ, I am called an Evangelist with a prophetic anointing. In all honesty, I am still feeling chills right now. I ended up sharing my vision with a friend, Pastor Mary. She agreed that he was giving me specific instructions. I could tell because it was like he had my full attention and I was mesmerized with what he was saying.

I spent some time questioning God after knowing what I had seen asking myself was that real. Then one day I picked up a book that was in my home with a picture in it. I heard God say open the book. When I opened the book, I saw a stories about other prophets like Ezekiel, Moses, & John that also saw the same vision of God seated on the throne. The deep thing is that the picture someone illustrated was the exact same thing that I saw. Chills ran through my spine as I cried again. I must have opened and reclosed that book to that page I don't remember how many times. I can remember seeing a bible verse as I read the part of the book near the illustration to see what this was all about. The verse in the book read, "Come up here, and I will show you things". The full verse can be found in (Revelations 4:1) The book of Revelations reveals when John saw this vision also. My God! It was as if God was saying if you exit the natural realm and spend time with me in the spirit realm, then I can show you things.

I received a third confirmation. My sister does artwork. She had just finished with some portraits that she made. I must have visited my mom and she was there. She began to show me some of her portraits. This one picture stood out to me. When I picked it up and read it, the words read "Come up here, and I will show you things" You know we just don't know sometimes just how much the Lord is using us. Lord have mercy! Lord I don't need to see anymore confirmations! You have my full attention! Chills went up my spine again. All I can say at this point is that God is real. Whether people decide to believe this or not, I know what I saw. There is a spirit realm and earth realm and if we come out of the carnal mind, he will show us things.

Encounter #2

The Lord has me really sharing intimate moments in this book that I have only shared with a few. There was a time around that same time that I was shown the vision of the throne that I saw a bush burning as I was sleeping. It was just a quick flash and went away but I bet you when I woke up I did not need to question what I had seen this time. There was no need to go through that again. Again I wondered what that was all about. When God shows me things I instantly know what he is saying but there are those other times that he wants me to seek him. I thought about the burning bush and of course I needed to search the scriptures. God has got away of making me study his word. I realized that during the time of the burning bush that this was the time where Moses lead his people out of bondage. So Lord what does this have to do with me? At this point in my life, my family had stopped going to church. There were people in my family that needed to receive Christ. Earlier in this book remember when I wrote about the time when I started going to church by myself. I can remember after seeking him that he told me that I was like Moses. God's specific words were that I would help lead my family out of bondage. In all honesty, I was flattered but scared. This felt like too much of a mantle for me. I did not want this but in time I accepted this. You see, I was the lamp that he chose to intercede on those family member's behalf. To this day, I still carry that mantle but I thank God that one by one God is reeling those family members in. My family members are receiving Christ one by one. Some of them are still fighting but I am still praying. When we stand in gap for our family, God honors our prayers. (In Mother Bynum's words) I heard her say this once in a Youtube video I watched. The video is a must watch. She visited TBN while Waunita Bynum was still hosting the show at that time and spoke of this very subject. With that said in mind, stand in the gap for your family members. We cannot make them do the right things but we can sure petition God on their behalf.

Encounter #3

There was a day many years ago that my children had gone somewhere with my husband. This was an opportunity to catch up on some sleep. Anybody that knows me knows that I am an everyday busy body in the since that I am always up to something. If I am not planning something, I am coming up with a new line of jewelry, fashion, or something. I remember lying in my bed and of course at some point, I fell asleep. The best way that I can explain what happened to me is to say that I was sleep but could feel that someone was in the room with me. In other words, I was sleep but could feel God's presence. I could feel God just saying rest in me. It was a sleep that was one of the sweetest sleeps that I had ever felt in life.

Sometimes my mind is just full of stuff. Even though the Lord had me in rest mode the enemy tried to come in and make me think about business, a new idea or something. Even when we are sleep, our minds are still subconsciously working. The truth is that I never sleep on my back but this time I did. All I can remember is trying to get up thinking that I needed to get up and start working on something. My eyes were still closed but I could feel myself trying to get up. Just as I lifted my body up, a hand pushed my body back down in my chest and a voice said rest in me. I knew it was God. I never opened my eyes, and all I know is that I was knocked out for a while in the presence of God. I hope I am not scaring my readers. I am just lead to share.

Encounter #4

By this time I had only four children. I can remember trying to do bible study with my children. My children were playing and clowning so bad that I could not get their attention. I can remember getting frustrated with them. All I remember is that God spoke to me and said I will get their attention. He said that they were getting ready to experience my presence. This happened so fast. I remember saying and screaming to them ok you all keep on playing but God is getting ready to do something. All of a sudden, we heard a knock at the door. I knew it wasn't my husband. I know God does not mean for us to fear but I was shaken. I went over to the door and saw no one on the other side of the door. I am laughing now as I am typing but this is all true. This was not our imagination. We all heard the knock and if any ask those children they will all say the same thing to this day. All they could say was momma we are scared. I looked at them and simply said that I told you all that this was not something to play with. He got their attention and I was able to carry on. God told me early in my life to teach my children the bible and the things of the spirit. I was being obedient and they were being disobedient. God had my back didn't he?☺

Encounter #5

I mentioned earlier that my husband and I got married in a church with just the pastor present, my husband, and I. The church was very quiet. It was almost too quiet. I can remember hearing what I thought was just a crack or something in the air conditioner. So I thought! It was years later that that it was revealed to us through a prophetic word that the crack we heard was the presence of God. The prophet looked at us both and asked the question. Do you remember a sound in the church that sounded like a crack? My husband instantly said yes. The prophet then said that this was the presence of the Lord putting his seal on the unity. Yes the enemy has tried to destroy our marriage may times but most of the time if I need to question whether or not we should be together, I think about that prophetic word. Whatever the Lord joins together let nothing or no one separate.

I could go on and on but I won't. I will write more books about my experiences later. I have always been a quiet spoken person that is very observant of my surroundings. I've often been overlooked, misunderstood, and sometimes even considered to be strange. God's people are peculiar people. There were many times that I shared what I knew was a word from God with the people that are the closest to me to only be rejected. If I don't get the spirit of intimidation from them, I can tell for whatever the reason that they do not receive what I am saying. Not every prophet will say that what they believe is a word from God but it does not mean that they aren't speaking prophetically. This is how people miss God sometimes. Often God has shown me something and I can casually bring this up as being lead by the spirit in a conversation with that person and almost instantly God shows me that they are rejecting the prophet. The journey is not easy for those that are chosen. To reject a true prophet, is rejecting God. It is well with me though! God prepares us for the journey. Though it's an uphill journey, it is one that is a rewarder to those that diligently seek him.

## My Everyday Prayer

Father in the name of Jesus, I thank you for your many blessings and for waking me up this morning. I ask that you order my steps that your will is done. I pray that people are drawn to your presence through me. I pray that you would use me to deliver and set the captives free. I pray that you would go before me in the presence of mine enemies. Lord guard my heart and mind that I will do what is right in the sight of you. I pray that you would save the unsaved, remember those that are incarcerated, and that your ministers of God will teach a true word. I pray for every loved one, friend, and family member. You know what they stand in need of before they ask. I believe in Jesus name that the prayers that I have prayed are already done. In Jesus name! Amen!

# A Call to Salvation

~~~~~~~~~~~~~

    I could not finish this book without extending an opportunity for my readers to receive Christ in their life. Many feel that to be saved means a boring life full of rules and no fun. I can truly say that I have so much fun in Christ now that I can't wait to see what God will do next in my life. Satan will not stop trying to kill, steal, and destroy because a person becomes saved but isn't it a blessing to know that we do not have to go through anything alone? No matter what comes our way, he's got our back. The enemy may raise his head but we will soon see his day of destruction.

    Now that I am saved, I have peace and joy unspeakable. I know that I am not alone, and I can help others become a part of his realm. Join me in this journey by receiving this invitation to Christ. Please if you are not sincerely ready do not waste your or Gods time. God honors a sincere heart. You can open up your heart by asking him to come in and take total control over your life. Acknowledge him as being Lord and savior over your life and believe that he died on the cross for your sins. Repenting from sin is admitting that there is sin and being sorrowful about those sins by turning from them. Does this mean that we will be perfect and not sin? No because all have sinned. We must strive everyday to do the right things and when we fall short, we should ask for forgiveness and begin again. Now does this give us a license to do just keep on doing the same things over and over again? I don't advise this because we have to deal with the consequences of our sin. Thank God that his mercy endureth forever. Grace is pretty good too!

I do not feel that we have to go to church every Sunday but I do feel that a true bible based church will help. When I first started learning about the word of God I actually taught myself from children's bible story books and I am not ashamed because I just did not understand the bible. I made sure that after I read the stories that the stories lined up with what is in the bible. Children's story books just explain things easier.

I feel that each person should study the scriptures for themselves. I always pray before I read his word. I pray for wisdom and understanding. I also pray that the carnal mind is removed so that I can receive in the spirit. If we do not study his word a person could be teaching us that the sky is green. Now that we have received, we must give. As we were lead to Christ we can tell somebody else about Jesus!

# Summary

~~~~~~~~~

This book is not a tell all. It is an act of obedience. Honestly this was a little hard for me because I am such a private person. When I received a word from him through a prophet that said that it is time for me to stop hiding, I knew what God was saying. I believe that not only does God want his glory to be revealed through this book but that he wanted people to get a strong since of just who I am in Christ. To best describe me I would say that I am a very humble, compassionate, & spiritually gifted person. I am not in any way judgemental but I do believe in giving people the truth according to the gospel. If God gives it to me, I do not have a problem with sharing truth with others. Many do not receive me but they did not receive Jesus either.

My heart is for the people and not only am I spiritually gifted but I enjoy taking care of the needs of his people. I believe the scriptures that say that only a few people will actually make it in. I urge readers today to get saved if you are not and share the gospel with friends and family members. Many people that confess do not possess. Some of the same people that we see in church from Sunday to Sunday including pastors, preachers, leaders, and so forth will bust hell wide open. I urge you if you haven't read the book "The Divine Revelation of Hell", to read it. Mary K. Baxter is the author. My husband bought books just to give to people. Look her up on the web and on Youtube. I read the entire book in two days. The contents were enough to make me want to stay saved. If you are a person that has not had the opportunity to be baptized in your church talk with your pastor.

    Please do not be like me and live in the belly of that big fish like I did for so many years. We do not have much time left on this earth. People say that there will be a time when the devil is loose on the earth. Well I believe that time is now. Our children are falling by the wayside. They are practicing witchcraft, cutting themselves, the music industry is evil, people seem to be whatever sexual preference they want, and the world is just getting wickeder and wickeder. To whom much is given, much is required. Freely we have received, and now freely we must give a word of God to people who desire to receive him. I had to realize that this is not about me but about obedience and doing the will of my father. I would like to end by saying whatever is holding you back from your destiny, Let It Go!!!

www.ingramcontent.com/pod-product-compliance
Lightning Source LLC
LaVergne TN
LVHW051154080426
835508LV00021B/2616